THE
CROSS
CHURCH

ADVENT is derived from the Latin word "adventus" meaning "coming." For centuries, Advent has marked the beginning of the liturgical year in many Christian church traditions.

By the 6th century, Advent became associated with the coming of Christ - both reflecting back on Jesus' first coming 2,000 years ago and looking forward to His promised second coming. Today, the Advent season lasts about four weeks and is meant to be a time of holy anticipation, reflection, and expectation as we celebrate Christ's birth and eventual return.

# JOURNEY WITH US

As we enter the Advent season and anticipate celebrating the birth of our Savior, we are pleased to share with you this special series of Advent devotionals, meaningful reflections crafted by members of The Cross Church faith family who share their thoughts and experiences surrounding the Advent themes of

# HOPE, FAITH, JOY, and PEACE

Arrange your own advent setting and use this booklet to prepare your heart for the coming of our Savior and Lord, Jesus Christ. You will need a wreath, three purple candles and one pink candle.

The wreath is a circle having no beginning and no end, representing eternal life found only in Jesus Christ. Evergreen signifies the unending love of God. Four candles represent four weeks until Christmas day.

We pray these heartfelt insights draw you closer to our Lord this Christmas season with a renewed awe of the miraculous word made flesh as we await the arrival of our glorious King.

Sunday, December 1, 2024

# HOPE

## Prophecy Candle

As we light the first candle, we remember Christ is the hope of the world. We wait for the coming of Christmas day, but most of all we wait with hope and excitement for the second coming of Christ and the everlasting life we have been promised when we believe in Him. While we wait, it is a time for repentance, prayer and examination. John the Baptist proclaimed, "Prepare the way of the Lord; make his paths straight." A king rides on smooth and straight roads. Let's begin this advent season by straightening the roads of our hearts as Christians have done for thousands of years in anticipation of the return of our Lord and King.

Read: Isaiah 40:3-5 and Matthew 3:1-12

Sing: O Come, O Come, Emmanuel

# Monday, December 2, 2024

WRITTEN BY KEITH GRAY

For the grace of God has appeared, bringing salvation for all people, training us to renounce ungodliness and worldly passions, and to live self-controlled, upright, and godly lives in the present age, waiting for our blessed hope, the appearing of the glory of our great God and Savior Jesus Christ.
**Titus 2:11-13**

"When will they get here?" said the 10 year old boy on his birthday. "I can't wait anymore!"

If you've ever waited for the guests to arrive at your child's birthday party, you understand the urgency of this situation. Seconds feel like minutes, minutes like hours, and so on. Their friends arrive bearing gifts and the excitement that comes with hope of the fun that is about to be had. Children around the world agree: it's worth the wait.

The experience of God's people has also been one of waiting and expectation and hope. From the very beginning, when Adam and Eve introduced sin into the world and God promised to send a rescuer to save people from the ravaging effects of that sin, the redemption countdown began. By the time of Jesus' birth, God's people had grown accustomed to waiting. Ever since God had clearly designated Abraham's family as the line through which He would send a Redeemer, His people had watched for this Messiah, always hoping that His arrival would be right around the corner. After the prophet Malachi, there was 400 years of silence. Had God abandoned His people? Had their rebellion reached His limits of forgiveness?

God broke this silence first by sending John the Baptist to prepare the way. Then He split the silence wide open with another baby — a baby who wouldn't just patch up a broken world but would bring salvation for all people!

We know about the story of Jesus the Messiah and how His story on earth ended...for the moment. But knowing about the story is not enough, for we were created to know the Author of the story.

During this Advent season, you are likely waiting for something. Perhaps it is a good test result from a doctor or a phone call from an estranged loved one, or even an answer to your prayers. As with God's people through the ages, our human experience is also defined by hopeful waiting. Paul's words above were written as an encouragement to persevere. Not only do we have hope, we have a blessed hope. A hope that will wipe away every tear and make all things new. A hope in One who not only has already come and gone but who will come again.

What are you hoping for most during this Advent season?

## Today's Prayer

Father, we come to you now confessing that we are not good at waiting. And though we are impatient, it is because we know that You have so much more in store for us. Forgive us and help us remain faithful and true to our calling, to spread the fame of Jesus to the world. We thank you for the salvation we have in Jesus and we thank you for the blessed hope we have in His return. You truly are the giver of the greatest gifts, the greatest is our Savior Jesus Christ, Amen.

BLESSED SAVIOR

WE ADORE THEE

WE THY LOVE AND GRACE

PROCLAIM

THOU ART MIGHTY

THOU ART HOLY

GLORIOUS

IS THY MATCHLESS NAME

GLORIOUS, GLORIOUS

GLORIOUS IS

THY NAME

O' LORD

# Tuesday, December 3, 2024
WRITTEN BY BRANDON FROSCH

Now may the God of hope fill you with all joy and peace as you believe so that you may overflow with hope by the power of the Holy Spirit.
**Romans 15:13**

When faced with an undesirable task, my wife and I often like to copy a joke from the TV series *How I Met Your Mother*, "That sounds like a job for future Lisa and Brandon." "Yeah, let's let those two take care of this!" Unfortunately, as attractive as putting things off until later may seem, it almost always ends with us cursing our past selves, "Come on, past Lisa and Brandon!"

Interestingly enough, the way we view time can have a great deal to do with the language we speak. Some languages such as Japanese, Finnish, Mandarin, and German very closely link the present and the future linguistically. Instead of a student saying "I will be an engineer one day" as we would in English, these futureless languages would translate closer to "I am an engineer one day." This subtle shift in language recognizes that if "I am an engineer," I should do the things that engineers do. UCLA Economist Keith Chen theorized that by speaking about the future and the present in the same words, they create a mental link about how what they do in the present affects the future. He even found that people who speak these languages put about 31% more money into savings each year than a comparative person who speaks a "futured" language.

So, what does this have to do with hope? Romans says that the God of hope will fill us with joy and peace as we believe. Our hope is based in the future on the promises of God through Jesus Christ. He has promised us life eternal, that we will not perish, and that none can snatch us from His hand (John 10:28). He has promised to never leave us nor forsake us, that even when we are faithless, God remains faithful (Hebrews 13:5, 2 Timothy 2:13) Now, because of this hope He has given for our future, we may live in joy and peace. Romans goes on to remind us that "If God is for us, who can be against us?" Hope is therefore tomorrow's effect on how we live our lives today.

Now, before we simply reduce our hope to a logical conclusion, let's be honest. Sometimes our circumstances cloud our judgment, stoke our fears, and cause us to fear and doubt. Sometimes we are tossed about like waves on the ocean. Our faith wavers, and we feel anything but peaceful and joyful. In times like these, thank God for His Holy Spirit. Jesus declared that in this world we would have trouble. But, take heart, because as we believe, our hope in God comes from God by the power of the Spirit and is completely separate from any external circumstances. He has overcome the world, and our future is secure in Him.

Let us allow the hope we have in God's promises to radiate joy and peace through the way we live our daily lives.

## Today's Prayer

Our gracious heavenly Father, God of hope who grants us joy and peace beyond all possible understanding, we bow before you. God, you never leave us, but sometimes we lose sight of you. We allow ourselves to get buried under the weight of our circumstances. Father, shift our focus from our trials and troubles to focus on your promises and the hope they bring. Your peace is supernatural. Your joy is lasting. Thank you for loving us though we could never deserve it, Amen.

MAY THE GOD OF

HOPE

FILL YOU WITH ALL

JOY AND PEACE

AS YOU TRUST IN HIM.

SO THAT YOU MIGHT OVERFLOW WITH

HOPE

BY THE POWER OF THE

HOLY SPIRIT

# Wednesday, December 4, 2024

WRITTEN BY RICK DIRKSE

I pray also that the eyes of your heart may be enlightened in order that you may know the hope to which he has called you, the riches of his glorious inheritance in the saints.
**Ephesians 1:18**

Have you listened to the news lately or read the newspaper? We live in a world that is confused, deceived, led astray and without hope. But I have good news for you! Ephesians 1:18 declares that we "the saints" can know "the hope" to which we have been called.

God's word declares to us today, we "the saints" have HOPE!!! God's word declares to us today, we "the saints" can know and experience this hope even in this crazy world! This is good news this advent season.

Why do we have hope? We have hope because we "the saints" have believed and trusted in the Lord Jesus Christ. What is this hope the scriptures speak of? Ephesians 1:3-14 clearly describes our hope:

- vs 3) We have spiritual blessings in the heavenly places.
- vs 4) We are blameless before God.
- vs 7) We have forgiveness of our sins.
- vs 8) We have wisdom and insight.
- vs 9) We know the mystery of His will.
- vs 10) We participate in God's plan to unite all things in Him and on earth.
- vs 11) We have an inheritance.
- vs 13) We have been sealed with the Holy Spirit of promise as a guarantee to all of this.

Wow, what hope we have! Don't believe the news: believe the truth, the real good news, the Bible!

How can we understand this hope today?

### Enlightenment > Knowledge > Wisdom > Understanding > Hope

To understand the prayer that Paul prays for us in Ephesians 1:18, we must first understand when the Bible speaks of the heart. It is not only the organ that pumps blood to your body.

The heart of the Bible is much more than that. It is the center of our spirit, soul, and body. It is the inner part of a person that houses our will, mind, emotions, and understanding. It is the part of you created by God that makes you uniquely you.

To prove this, the Bible has hundreds of scriptures about the heart. Here are a few:

**Proverbs 3:5-6, Proverbs 4:23, Psalm 86:11, 1 Samuel 16:7**

The Bible tells us to trust the Lord with all our heart. The Bible tells us to guard our hearts. The Bible tells us to not have divided hearts. Why? The Bible tells us that God does not look at the outward appearance, but God looks at the heart. Clearly these scriptures are not just speaking about the organ that pumps blood to our bodies. The heart of a person is much more than that. The heart of a person is the place of man where we know God and He knows us. Paul prayed for the Ephesians that the Holy Spirit of wisdom, revelation, and knowledge (vs 17) would enlighten the eyes of their hearts so that they can know, understand, and live the hope described in Ephesians 1:3-14.

## Today's Prayer

My prayer is that if they have not believed and trusted in you that they will. I pray that you will draw them to you and that they will believe in the Lord Jesus Christ and that the Spirit of wisdom, revelation and knowledge would enlighten their hearts to the hope you have for them. I also pray for the saints who lack wisdom and understanding, that you will give it to them so in their hearts, they may know you and be known and encouraged by you in the hope you have for them. We love you and are thankful for your love of us, AMEN

I PRAY THAT THE

EYES OF YOUR HEART

MAY BE ENLIGHTENED.
THAT YOU MAY KNOW

THE HOPE

TO WHICH WE'RE CALLED.
THAT YOU MAY KNOW

THE RICHES

OF HIS GLORY.
THAT YOU MAY KNOW

THE GREATNESS,

THE GREATNESS OF HIS POW'R
TOWARD US WHO BELIEVE.
I PRAY THAT THE

EYES OF YOUR HEART

MAY BE ENLIGHTENED.
MAY HE OPEN THE EYES OF YOUR HEART.

# Thursday, December 5, 2024

WRITTEN BY ALLEN STROUD

But they who wait for the Lord shall renew their strength; they shall mount up with wings like eagles; they shall run and not be weary; they shall walk and not faint.
**Isaiah 40:31**

## CONSIDER GOD

In the clutter and chaos of the coming Christmas season, in the press of a world gone crazy, confronted on every side by distress, discontent and disruption, we feel overwhelmed, worn thin and weary. We are tempted to lock the door, climb into bed, and pull the covers over our heads to escape the assault. We know that such behavior ultimately will not help. So, we trudge through our days exhausted and joyless.

Until, like Isaiah, we consider God. A powerful God who fashioned the universe out of nothing. A creative God who placed the stars, oceans, and dry land in place. A sovereign God who rules with justice. A caring God who levels mountains and fills valleys. A generous God who gave us His only Son. A gentle God who deeply loves His children. A mighty God who conquers evil. An everlasting God who longs to welcome us into eternity.

When we step aside to consider God, wait in His calm and quiet presence, and recognize who He is, hope stirs in our hearts. He is the One who enables us to confront the daily challenges of this world. He strengthens, empowers, renews, revives, and reinvigorates us. Not just to walk but to run. Not just to get to the end of another day but to soar with joy. We are not alone in this battle: God is with us!

We cannot imagine, nor can we anticipate the full complexity of life, but God can. God knows. When we put our confidence and hope in God and wait for God's direction, we find the best path through the darkness. His yoke is easy. His burden is light. We find we can move forward in God's strength. We do not feel faint any longer...we feel energized. We do not feel weary... we feel excited. Not in our strength. Not by ourselves. But in accord with our Lord and Savior, in the strength of the Body of Christ, empowered by the Holy Spirit. We will face each day with joy and strength. We will see God at work in our lives, communities and world.

How will you wait for the Lord this season?

## Today's Prayer

Almighty God, help us step aside from the world's chaos and spend time in Your precious presence. Help us to see things from Your perspective, hear Your voice, and trust and follow You alone. Remind us of Your unfailing, everlasting love. Lead us beside still waters in paths of righteousness that we may serve You all the days of our lives, Amen.

# STRENGTH

WILL RISE AS WE WAIT UPON THE LORD

OUR GOD YOU REIGN

## FOREVER

OUR HOPE, OUR STRONG DELIV'RER

YOU ARE THE EVERLASTING GOD

YOU DO NOT **FAINT**

YOU DO NOT GROW WEARY

YOU ARE THE EVERLASTING GOD

YOU ARE THE **DEFENDER**

OF THE WEAK, YOU COMFORT

THOSE IN NEED, YOU LIFT US UP ON

## WINGS LIKE EAGLES

# Friday, December 6, 2024

WRITTEN BY DENNIS DAVIDSON

[18] Behold, the eye of the Lord is on those who fear him, on those who hope in his steadfast love, [19] that he may deliver their soul from death and keep them alive in famine.

**Psalm 33:18-19**

The simplistic visual of this verse would be one of God peering down from His balcony suite in Heaven watching and observing as events unfold in our lives. That is much too limiting.

God's perspective on our lives is infinite and He is always orchestrating our circumstances for personal good. The big word is "omnipresence." God is always with us and is in full control. Wherever we go, we will find ourselves completely protected because of God's presence. He has a master plan for our lives and has it all mapped out.

This thought is repeated in 2 Chronicles 16:9: "For the eyes of the LORD run to and fro throughout the whole earth, to show Himself strong on behalf of those whose heart is loyal to Him." God's eye on us means more than a simple awareness. It means He is constantly looking to protect, sustain, and bring us through the difficulties we encounter every day. Because of His sovereign knowledge and foresight of all things, we can rest assured that God is still in control.

This is the true hope of believers. The Greek term for "hope" in today's verse means "an eager, confident expectation." Hoping in God will never lead us into despair because we can be confident of His master plan and steadfast love. He has a future planned for us that is full of hope.

Charles Swindoll explains it this way: "You're God's personal project of character growth. That means you can rejoice even more because God never gives up on His project. He always has His eye on you, cultivating your character through tribulations."

"And I am sure of this, that he who began a good work in you will bring it to completion at the day of Jesus Christ." (Philippians 1:6 ESV).

Paul took it even further explaining our hope is alive. "Praise be to the God and Father of our Lord Jesus Christ! In his great mercy he has given us new birth into a living hope through the resurrection of Jesus Christ from the dead...." (1 Peter 1:3 NIV).

Our hope is alive because Jesus is alive! Our living hope is solid and secure. "We have this hope as an anchor for the soul, firm and secure" (Hebrews 6:19–20 CSB).

God loves us and for this reason He gave us Jesus Christ to be our Savior, our salvation, our Living Hope!

Reflect back over this past year and think about all that has happened to you—good and bad—and be cognizant of it as part of God's eye on you. "For we are God's masterpiece. He has created us anew in Christ Jesus, so we can do the good things he planned for us long ago" (Ephesians 2:10).

## Today's Prayer

Heavenly Father, thank You for sustaining us in Your grace through times of suffering, misery, and disappointment—as well as the good—as part of your master plan of our lives. Thank you for keeping your eye on us and safeguarding us through it all. Thank you for giving us our living hope which is built on nothing less than Jesus' blood and righteousness. In the loving and gracious name of Jesus Christ, Amen.

OH LORD YOU'RE

# BEAUTIFUL

YOUR FACE

IS ALL I SEEK

AND WHEN YOUR EYES

ARE ON THIS CHILD

# YOUR GRACE

ABOUNDS TO ME

# Saturday, December 7, 2024

WRITTEN BY AUSTIN BRATTON

Let us hold fast the confession of our hope without wavering, for he who promised is faithful. And let us consider how to stir up one another to love and good works, not neglecting to meet together, as is the habit of some, but encouraging one another, and all the more as you see the Day drawing near.

**Hebrews 10:23-25**

We need each other. Intuitively we know this.

The world organizes itself in groups: sports teams, business teams, families, churches, service organizations. Each group has a purpose, a mission. Sometimes that mission is clearly defined (e.g., win the championship!), and sometimes less so (e.g., I doubt many families have a clearly defined family mission statement!). Those goals and purposes are motivated by something, and the more closely the goals of the group motivate both the team and the individuals within it, the more successful that group will be. When any person doesn't do their part or does so half-heartedly, the overall mission suffers.

Here in Hebrews, the writer ties what individual Christians do (the what, the mission) to the motivation (the once-for-all sacrifice of Christ on the cross). Hebrews 10:1-18 explains that what the Old Testament sacrificial system could never do (take away sins for good), Jesus did by offering himself once-for-all to bring us back into right relationship with God. Given this backdrop, the author gives two big motivators for the instructions that follow:

- **Hebrews 10:19-20**. We now have confidence to enter the holy places (i.e., God's presence!) by the blood of Jesus (i.e., his sacrifice for us!) >> Jesus is the way to the Father (John 14:6)
- **Hebrews 10:21**. We have a great high priest over the house of God >> Jesus is our mediator directly to the Father (Romans 8:34)

In light of these great truths, the author now calls his listeners (and us) to the following:

1. Draw near to God confidently (22)
2. Hold to hope unwaveringly (23)
3. Stir up one another to love and good works habitually (24-25)

Jesus gives us access directly to the Father. It is Christ's faithfulness by which we confidently come into God's presence. We have a restored relationship with the Almighy Creator, now our Loving Father.

When we confess Jesus as Lord (king, ruler, chief of our lives) and believe in our hearts that God raised him from the dead, we are saved (Romans 10:9-10) and have hope both in this life and the next (1 Corinthians 15:19-20). Because our perseverance is based on Christ's faithfulness, not our perfection, our hope can be unwavering.

Yet, we don't always feel this confident, unwavering hope do we? We encounter challenges, we face doubts, we may be fearful. That's where we need each other. God has given us one another to encourage each other, to habitually spur each other on to love one another, to do good to everyone, and especially to those of the household of faith (Gal 5:9-10).

How can you hold to Jesus this Advent season together in community with others? Who needs your encouragement? Whose encouragement do you need? Reach out in love.

## Today's Prayer

Lord Jesus, thank you for making a way for us to be reconciled to God. Thank you for giving us an everlasting hope that endures throughout all eternity. I rejoice that I am now a child of God with full access to the Father. Thank you for giving us one another—other believers in the Church—to encourage, and to love, and to pursue good together in community. This Advent Season, I pray that we would all recommit to showing the world that we are Christians by the way we love each other just as you said. Let us hold unwaveringly to the hope that we will one day spend eternity with you in heaven. Come quickly, Lord Jesus.

# RISE UP
O CHURCH OF GOD!

HAVE DONE WITH LESSER THINGS

# GIVE HEART
AND MIND, AND SOUL, AND STRENGTH

TO SERVE THE

# KING OF KINGS
LIFT HIGH THE CROSS OF CHRIST

TREAD WHERE HIS FEET HAVE TROD

# AS FOLL'WERS
OF THE SON OF MAN

RISE UP

# O CHURCH OF GOD!

Sunday, December 8, 2024

# FAITH

## Bethlehem Candle

As we light the second purple candle, the Faith candle, we also remember the birth of Jesus and why God sent His son to save us. It is called the "Bethlehem Candle," as a reminder of Mary and Joseph's journey to Bethlehem, The City of David and the birthplace of our Lord and Saviour. It symbolizes the preparations made to receive and cradle the Christ child. Bethlehem is the place where a humble couple put their faith in God to follow Him on an unwanted journey, at an inconvenient time, to a tiny, insignificant town.

Read: Genesis 3, Matthew 1:18-25, Luke 2:1-7 and John 3:16

Sing: O Little Town of Bethlehem and Away in a Manger

# Monday, December 9, 2024

WRITTEN BY ALLEN STROUD

Now faith is the assurance of things hoped for, the conviction of things not seen. For by it the people of old received their commendation. By faith we understand that the universe was created by the word of God, so that what is seen was not made out of things that are visible.

**Hebrews 11:1-3**

In Hebrews there is an element which is regarded as essential to the Christian life, and that is faith. It is what makes the Christian different from the non-Christian. Henry David Thoreau once said, "If I seem to walk out of step with others, it is because I am listening to another drumbeat." That is an appropriate description of faith: Christians walk as though listening to another drumbeat.

This chapter centers on what faith is. Faith is greatly misunderstood and there are many peculiar ideas of what it is. Faith is not positive thinking. Faith is not a hunch that is followed. Faith is not hoping for the best, hoping that everything will turn out alright. Faith is not a feeling of optimism. Faith is none of these things, though all of them have been identified as faith.

What is faith then? Faith begins with things hoped for, that is, it starts with a sense of discontent. You can never have much faith unless you are dissatisfied with the way you are now and are longing for something better. That is why, all through the Bible, the great enemy of faith is a complacent spirit, an attitude of self-satisfaction with the status quo. But if you are dissatisfied, if you are looking for something better, then you are in a position to exercise faith.

Then comes the conviction of things not seen — not only a desire for something better, but an awareness of something else: That is faith. It means we become aware that we are surrounded by an invisible kingdom, that which is seen is not the whole explanation of life, there are realities which cannot be seen or touched, and yet which are as real and as vital as anything we can see. Luke speaks of a righteous and faith-filled man named Simeon who had patiently waited his whole life hoping for the consolation of Israel. Praise the Lord, his faith was realized when the Holy Spirit revealed to him that he would not experience death until he had seen the Messiah, the Christ, and in fact, as ordained by the Spirit, was able to hold Jesus, the Christ child in his arms, proclaiming, "Lord, now you are letting your servant depart in peace, according to Your word; for my eyes have seen your salvation..."

Are you a person of faith? Is there a hunger for something better in your life? Is there a conviction that God is ready to answer your cry? In fact, he has already answered it, in Christ.

What is giving you a feeling of discontent this Advent season and what is the better thing you are longing for?

## Today's Prayer

Father, thank you for the revelation of what faith is. How I feel the need of it as I live in the midst of a confused and hopeless society. Grant me the simple faith of a child and teach me to live according to it.

Amen.

WHEN I GAZE INTO THE

# NIGHT SKIES

AND SEE THE WORK OF YOUR FINGERS

THE MOON AND STARS SUSPENDED

# IN SPACE

OH WHAT IS MAN THAT YOU ARE MINDFUL OF HIM

YOU HAVE GIVEN MAN A CROWN OF

# GLORY AND HONOR

AND HAVE MADE HIM A LITTLE LOWER THAN THE ANGELS

YOU HAVE PUT HIM IN CHARGE OF

# ALL CREATION

THE BEASTS OF THE FIELD THE BIRDS OF THE AIR

THE FISH OF THE SEA BUT WHAT IS MAN

# OH WHAT IS MAN

THAT YOU ARE MINDFUL OF HIM

O LORD OUR GOD

# THE MAJESTY

AND GLORY OF YOUR NAME

TRANSCENDS THE EARTH AND FILLS THE HEAVENS

# O LORD OUR GOD

LITTLE CHILDREN PRAISE YOU PERFECTLY

AND SO WOULD WE

# ALLELUIA

# Tuesday, December 10, 2024

WRITTEN BY HEATHER HABERMAN

Some trust in chariots, and some in horses;
But we will remember the name of the Lord our God.
**Psalm 20:7**

Have you ever been in conversation with someone that you didn't know very well, and they say, "Don't worry, trust me!" You are probably thinking, "Why should I trust you?"

We hardly ever stop and take inventory of our lives to think about what we put our trust in. We may not even realize that we have put our trust in anything at all. When trials come our way, a job loss for example, is the faith put in God that He will supply all our needs? Or is our faith and focus put in ourselves as we stress and worry about finding a new job and getting the bills paid? We tend to hyper focus on the stress and worry and leave God out of our struggle. When really, He wants to be involved in every part of it.

Ephesians 6:11 tells us to put on the whole armor of God, that you may be able to stand against the wiles of the devil. Jesus knew that we would deal with great adversity and trials, physically, mentally and spiritually. The human part of us leans towards the things of this world to put our faith and trust in, but we are called to put our trust in Him. Proverbs 3:5 'Trust in the LORD with all your heart, and do not lean on your own understanding.' Let me emphasize the 'ALL your heart'. Not some, not just the happy bits but ALL of it.

Trusting in the Lord is like reading a book and skipping ahead to the end to see what happens. We already know that He wins! Hallelujah! We already know that He came, He lived, and He died so that we could be with Him in Heaven. If we can trust that He loves us enough to die for us, can we not trust Him enough with the everyday, nitty gritty of our lives?

What are some areas that you have not given up to Him? If you have started a list in your head and it seems to be growing quickly, you are not alone. Many of us have not fully surrendered to Him. It can seem overwhelming at times and difficult to know where to start. The good news is... Jesus is not looking for perfection, He is looking for our surrender, so He can address what we are unwilling to let go of.

How can we fully surrender to Jesus?

## Today's Prayer

Heavenly Father, please prepare our hearts and our minds for the amazing things that come when we fully surrender to you. Remind us that you have already won the battle; that we can trust you with all that our lives bring no matter how difficult and how defeating they may feel. Help us to lay it down and along with the burden, allow us to lay down the worry that can overcome us. Let us rejoice in the knowledge that you will never forsake us. Thank you for your word, your love and your desire to walk beside us Lord.

In your precious and wonderful name Lord, Amen!

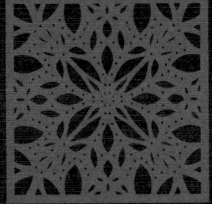

SOME TRUST IN
CHARIOTS AND SOME IN HORSES
BUT WE WILL REMEMBER
THE NAME OF OUR GOD, THE GOD OF
ISRAEL
HIS HAND IS MIGHTY HIS VICT'RY SURE
WE WILL REMEMBER THE
NAME OF OUR GOD
WE WILL TRUST IN THE LORD
THE GOD WHO
TOPPLED JERICHO
IS STILL AT WORK TODAY
AND MIGHTY WALLS STILL
CRUMBLE
FOR THOSE WHO TRUST AND PRAY,
THOUGH OBSTACLES
RISE HIGHER
AND HIDE THE PROMISED LAND,
THE OBSTACLES AND TOW'RING WALLS
STILL FALL
AT HIS COMMAND.

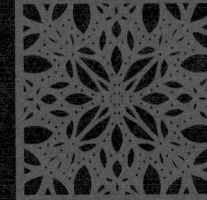

# Wednesday, December 11, 2024
WRITTEN BY THERESA EVETTS

So you see, faith by itself isn't enough. Unless it produces good deeds, it is dead and useless.
**James 2:17**

On a scale from 1-10, where do you rank in living out your faith? Maybe you rank yourself a 1. You do not believe in Jesus as Savior. You have not trusted Him to be your Lord. So, you do not have a faith to live out. Maybe you rank a 2 or 3. You have trusted Christ as Savior and Lord, but you have not professed your faith publicly. Your faith would not be obvious to anyone in the way that you live. If you rank yourself a 5, maybe your faith is apparent in front of close friends and family, but you are not sure how well you live out your faith beyond your inner circle. Perhaps you are a 10. You try to let everyone you encounter know that you are a believer in the Lord Jesus Christ. You do not want anyone to doubt your relationship with Him. The way you speak and act always demonstrates He is alive and actively working in and through your life. Depending on the day or perhaps even the moment, how well we are living out our faith can slide up or down the scale, so these are important questions we should reflect on and answer for ourselves daily.

James, thought to be the half-brother of Jesus and a leader of the first church in Jerusalem, writes a direct, no excuses letter filled with practical examples of how to pursue a life of genuine faith and holiness as a follower of Jesus Christ. He confronts those who "talk the Christian talk" but real life change is not evident. The way we speak and act should be living proof that we love and follow Jesus. This includes enduring trials with perseverance and faith, asking God for wisdom, taming our tongue, turning from sinful desires, living a life of humility rather than bitterness, envy and selfish ambition, serving and helping others, taking special care of orphans, widows and the poor as we would take care of ourselves.

But wait, aren't we saved by grace? Isn't salvation a gift from God and not something we can work for or earn? Yes. Salvation is a beautiful gift from God by grace through faith. It is admitting we are a sinner in need of a savior; believing Jesus is God's one and only son who lived a perfect life, loved us so much He died for our sin, and defeated death through His resurrection; and, confessing our belief in Him in our heart and with our mouth. James just helps clarify what should happen in our lives after a sincere conversion experience.

Good deeds, obedience and trust are the result and evidence of true faith. In contrast, a person who claims to know God but lacks evidence of a transformed life; such as ungodly behavior and a lack of "fruit" (love, joy, peace, patience, kindness, goodness, faithfulness, gentleness, and self-control...Galatians 5:22-23), has dead or useless faith. May our faith never be characterized as dead and useless.

Our good works are living proof of the Holy Spirit's transformation within us. Ask yourself, what good is my faith if no one knows about it or benefits from it? How will others experience Jesus and come to know Him personally if I am not willing to tell them about Him and demonstrate His loving kindness with faith-filled action? Let's not waste a single moment to show compassion, generosity, patience, self-control, truth in love, and all godliness as an expression of our transformed life in Jesus Christ.

## Today's Prayer

Dear Heavenly Father, we are so grateful for your free gift of salvation, but we understand while salvation is a gift of grace, it is proven in and by the things we say and do. Today, may we notice every opportunity to express to others our abundant, joy-filled, active faith in you. We want a faith that is alive and genuine, never dead or useless to your Kingdom. Continue to transform us into the likeness of Jesus Christ our Savior and Lord so that others will see you and come to know you through us. In the precious name of Jesus we pray.

Amen.

FAITH WITHOUT
WORKS
LIKE A SONG YOU CAN'T SING
IT'S ABOUT AS
USELESS
AS A SCREEN DOOR
ON A
SUBMARINE

# Thursday, December 12, 2024

WRITTEN BY DAN MARENGO

*So we are always of good courage. We know that while we are at home in the body we are away from the Lord, for we walk by faith, not by sight.*
**2 Corinthians 5:6-7**

I use Waze as my navigation app in an unfamiliar town or on a long road trip. I often get grief from people who travel with me because, at times, Waze will have me exit the highway unexpectedly or take me through a residential neighborhood when it seems there is a more direct route. However, without fail (so far!), there has always been an explanation for the unexpected detour - usually it's a traffic jam or a road closure. I couldn't see it coming, but Waze knew.

Faith is trusting in God even when we cannot see the road ahead. In 2 Corinthians 5:6-7, Paul reminds us that we live by faith, not by sight. Though we are present in our earthly bodies, our eternal home is in heaven with Christ. This means we often must walk forward without having the complete picture.

It takes great faith to follow God's calling when the path seems uncertain. But we can find comfort in knowing God guides our steps, even when we feel lost in the fog of life. He equips us for the tasks He has planned, though we may feel ill-prepared. He encourages to take the next step, even when we cannot yet see the destination.

Living by faith means clinging to God's promises when apprehension creeps in. It means praying for discernment when making difficult choices, trusting that God will make His will clear in due time. It means pursuing God's heart above earthly understanding, confident that He sees and knows more than we ever could.

Walking by faith inspires hope and builds character. As we lean on Him, God makes our faith stronger. Each step of trusting Him expands our capacity to believe Him more. Faith pleases God, for through it we acknowledge our dependence on Him. Let us have hearts willing to step forward in faith, even when our earthly eyes cannot perceive all that lies ahead. God rewards those who earnestly seek Him.

So today I challenge you:

1. Identify one area where you can walk in greater faith, even if you cannot yet see the outcome.

2. Take that step, trusting God is guiding you.

3. Draw near to Him in prayer and allow Him to build your faith.

## Today's Prayer

Dear God, teach me to walk by faith and not by sight. When my way feels unclear, grant me wisdom and discernment to take the next faith-filled step. Help me trust in Your perfect timing and plan, even when I cannot yet see. Empower me to follow You boldly, even when the path seems dim. Give me fresh confidence in Your unending faithfulness. Remind me that You equip those You call. Thank You for being with me always, guiding my steps according to Your purpose. In Jesus' Name, Amen.

WE WILL STAND AS
# CHILDREN
OF THE
## PROMISE
WE WILL FIX OUR EYES ON HIM
OUR SOUL'S
## REWARD
TILL THE RACE IS FINISHED
AND THE WORK IS
## DONE
WE WILL WALK BY FAITH
AND NOT BY SIGHT

# Friday, December 13, 2024
WRITTEN BY ALEX KLAGER

So faith comes from hearing, and hearing through the word of Christ.
**Romans 10:17**

"I can't hear God speaking in my life. Why doesn't He speak to me?"

There are many times when we speak to our children and they look at us with glossed over eyes. We ask them to do something around the house, they stare at us and have a difficult time following through on our instruction. God speaks to us in many ways like we do to our children. We are His children, adopted into His family through the sacrifice Jesus made on the cross. He gives us reminders of what He wants us to do in our lives, and wants us to trust Him. He speaks to us through His word. When we heard the gospel of Christ the first time, it changed us. It changed us because He alone can change us. He asks us to listen to Him. That proclamation of the gospel is so important in our lives, and we must carry that on to others so that they can hear the same.

When my wife and I were brought to Wylie, we didn't fully understand why God called us here. We knew He had a plan, and that we needed to trust him. It was scary, but we wanted to trust Him. We knew from previous times in our lives that God will make things happen that we could never fully understand. God spoke, we listened, and our lives were transformed and our faith grew. It is still growing to this day, and when we obey and trust in Him, He grows our faith.

What if you haven't heard His voice? You might have never heard His voice, or it has been a while since He has said anything to you. What can your faith do for you at this time?

God wants you to listen to Him, and hear what He has to say. He is a wonderful Father who is always there for us. He wants a relationship with Him that lasts forever. He wants you to trust in Him, always. We need Him so much.

God uses His word to change us, and He uses His followers to do the same. God speaks to us many times in our lives. The question is, are we listening? Faith is taking a step in His plan for you and not knowing where the next step will lead you, but trusting that God will direct you down the right path. He wants you to come to Him, with anything and everything. Faith is complete trust or confidence in God, even when you don't know what will happen next.

Faith doesn't come from years of experience at something, it comes from hearing the gospel and believing in what it says. When you open yourself to the truth that God brings you, it grows your faith. It is important for us to constantly seek His truth, so that it will grow our faith daily,

How can your faith be grown during this Advent season?

## KIDS CORNER
Ask your children these questions and listen to them. Spend time with them today and be intentional with this time you have with them. Remember, they belong to God and it is our responsibility to guide them to God, through His son Jesus. What does faith mean? Why does God want me to trust Him?

## Today's Prayer
Dear Father God, perfecter of our faith, may we seek your word each day. May we hear when you speak to us. May we trust in you completely, even when we don't know what the next step in our life will be, or what will happen. May you grow our faith, and help us in our faithlessness. God, how we need you today and every day. Use us to spread your message of the gospel to everyone you put in our lives. We need you, help us to trust in you more. It's in the mighty name of Jesus that we pray, Amen.

BY FAITH
WE HEAR AND WE BELIEVE THE GOSPEL.
BY FAITH
WE SEE AND WE RECEIVE HIS PROMISE.
JESUS
WELCOMES THE WEARY WHO CALL ON HIS NAME.
EVERY SINNER
WHO COMES TO THE CROSS WILL BE SAVED.
BY FAITH,
BY FAITH

# Saturday, December 14, 2024

WRITTEN BY DARIN REEVES

The apostles said to the Lord, "Increase our faith!"
**Luke 17:5**

Faith is acting as if something is so, even when it appears not to be so, in order that it might be shown to be so, simply because God said so.

"I can't do it daddy," cried the little boy as he lay on the street trying to get the bike off him. With the training wheels on, he could easily ride the bike, but his father knew he couldn't go through life with the training wheels on his bike. The little boy needed to trust his father that he wouldn't let go of him until he was able to balance the bike while peddling on his own. He needed faith in his father to hold him up, to guide him to ride without falling and trust that he would be right at his side. He needed to trust that his father would also be there to pick him up when he fell, ensure him that he could do it and help him back on the bike.

In Luke 17:5, the Disciples asked Jesus to increase their faith (ESV)...show us how to increase our Faith (NLT).

Jesus has just instructed the Disciples to show limitless forgiveness. Are they asking Jesus to increase their faith or are they more likely saying we can't do what you are asking us to do?

Jesus' response was directed at not the size of their faith but at the genuineness of their faith. The smallest amount of Faith is all that is needed to do what Jesus is asking them and us to do, the command to forgive others seven times and even more.

Jesus is telling His Disciples it is not the size of their Faith but the object of their Faith that will allow them to do greater things than even He. This requires a complete and intentional obedience to God's will.

Today, a lot of people relate Faith to Trust. Trust is the firm belief in the reliability, truth and ability or strength of someone or something. Trust is only as valuable as the thing to which it is tied to. Was the little boy putting his faith in his own ability to ride since he had done so with the training wheels or was his faith in his father to guide and teach him?

Hebrews 11 gives us God's directions on Faith. Now Faith is the assurance of things hoped for, the conviction of things not seen. Heb. 11:1 (ESV). Do we fully believe God is who He says He is, and He will do what He says?

When we ask Jesus to increase our Faith, what are we really asking or needing? Is it truly what we are putting our Faith in? Are we knowingly or unknowingly putting our Faith in things that we think are good — family, work, relationships — but should not be the main object of our Faith? Should our prayer be the cry of the father in Mark 9:24: I do believe but help me overcome my unbelief?

## Today's Prayer

Father God, thank You for Jesus, Your Word and Your Promises that are the object of my Faith. Help me to seek You daily and see Your love, grace and You in all things in my life. Lead me to grow in Jesus and show His love and grace to others I put my Faith in Jesus; He will never let me down. I pray these things in the Mighty and Powerful name of Jesus. Amen.

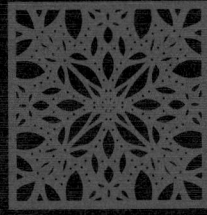

I DON'T HAVE TO BE THE

# STRONGEST

YOU ARE PERFECT IN MY WEAKNESS.

IF YOU CAN MOVE A MOUNTAIN

# WITH FAITH

LIKE A GRAIN OF MUSTARD SEED,

I WONDER WHAT YOU COULD DO

# WITH ME

YOU'RE THE GOD OF ALL CREATION,

YOU'RE THE KING ABOVE ALL KINGS.

# BUT ONLY YOU

CHOOSE A RUGGED CROSS TO RESCUE ME.

YOU'RE THE HEALER OF THE BROKEN,

# BY FAITH

I STILL BELIEVE.

YOU TOOK ON MY FLESH,

# CONQUERED DEATH

LORD YOU ARE MY VICTORY CAUSE

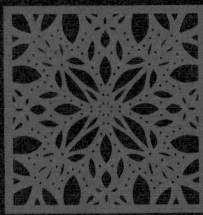
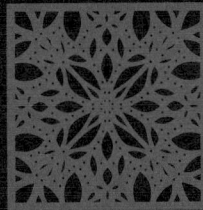

Sunday, December 15, 2024

# JOY

## Shepherd's Candle

The third candle we light is pink and symbolizes joy. It is also called the "Shepherd's Candle," taking us back to the joyful anticipation of the shepherds who journeyed to see Jesus in Bethlehem. It is meant to remind us of the joy that the world experienced at the birth of Jesus, and just like the shepherds who spread the word concerning what they had heard and seen, we must tell people about the good news of Jesus Christ. Unless we tell them, how will they hear and be saved?

Read: Luke 2:8-20

Sing: Joy to the World

# Monday, December 16, 2024

WRITTEN BY WILL HEATH

These things I have spoken to you, that my joy may be in
you, and that your joy may be full.
**John 15:11**

Joy-jitsu is a recognition that our mind, body, and soul are the literal battlefield of a cosmic struggle. As imperfect people, it can be difficult to avert our mind's focus and heart's affection from life's fleeting circumstances to God's present and eternal promises.

Paul's letter to the Galatians provides an interesting perspective on the internal spiritual tug of war raging inside us.

"But I say, walk by the Spirit and you will not carry out the desire of the flesh. **For the flesh sets its desire against the Spirit, and the Spirit against the flesh**; for these are in opposition to one another, so that you do not do the things you want." Galatians 5:16-17, LSB (emphasis added).

As people who have confessed Christ as Lord, what is the evidence the Spirit of God is claiming ground in this struggle? How can we tell we are maturing in our relationship with Christ?

"But the fruit of the Spirit is love, **JOY**, peace, patience, kindness, goodness, faithfulness, gentleness, self-control..." Galatians 5:22-23, LSB (emphasis added).

Along with the other qualities Paul lists, the presence of joy is the byproduct of the Spirit of God winning the spiritual struggle that rages within.

Joy provides calm delight, anchored in the soul's understanding and recognition that Jesus broke the bondage of sin, to which we were formerly a prisoner.

Joy is not tethered to circumstance. It is rooted in the eternal reality of Christ's victory over sin and death. Our happiness is no longer tied to the pursuit of temporary, fleeting experiences but to the eternal promises of God.

Positive emotions, not filtered through the work of Jesus, often disappear in the face of hardship. But for those who know the power of resurrection and find fellowship in the sufferings of Christ, joy settles the soul. (Philippians 3:10-11)

## Today's Prayer

Father, thank you for the revelation of what faith is. How I feel the need of it as I live in the midst of a confused and hopeless society. Grant me the simple faith of a child and teach me to live according to it.

Amen.

JESUS IS ALL THE WORLD TO ME

MY LIFE
MY JOY
MY ALL

HE IS MY STRENGTH FROM DAY TO DAY

WITHOUT

HIM

I WOULD FALL

WHEN I AM SAD, TO HIM I GO

NO OTHER ONE CAN CHEER ME SO

WHEN I AM SAD,
HE MAKES ME GLAD.

HE IS MY FRIEND

# Tuesday, December 17, 2024
WRITTEN BY SCOTT FINCH

Let the heavens be glad, and let the earth rejoice;
let the sea roar, and all that fills it;
let the field exult, and everything in it!
Then shall all the trees of the forest sing for joy
before the Lord, for he comes,
for he comes to judge the earth.
He will judge the world in righteousness,
and the peoples in his faithfulness.
**Psalm 96:11-13**

Psalm 96:11-13 exclaims with resounding joy as it calls upon all of creation to praise and worship the Lord. The psalmist's words urge the heavens, the earth, the sea, the fields, and even the trees of the forest to rejoice in the presence of God. This universal call to joy is rooted in the recognition of God's greatness, His rule over creation, and His righteous judgment. The psalmist's declaration of the Lord's splendor and majesty, and His reign as the righteous judge of the earth, inspires a deep sense of gratitude and reverence. The joy expressed in this passage is not limited to humans, but extends to all of creation, pointing to the unifying power of worship and praise. As we reflect on this passage, let us be reminded of the many blessings and the goodness of God that warrant such a joyful celebration.

The joy found in Psalm 96:11-13 is a powerful reminder of the abundant blessings and goodness of God that warrant our joyful response. It calls for a unifying celebration of worship and praise from all of creation and inspires us to share this joy with others. Let us heed the call to joy and respond with gratitude and reverence as we worship and praise the Lord.

So, how can we respond to this call to joy? Let us join in the chorus of creation and offer our heartfelt worship and praise to God, recognizing His greatness, His rule, and His righteousness.

Let us allow the joy of the Lord to overflow in our hearts and lives, impacting our attitudes, actions, and relationships. May we also share this joy with others by spreading God's fame and inviting them to join us in celebration.

## Today's Prayer
Heavenly Father, we are filled with joy as we contemplate Your greatness and Your rule over creation. Your splendor and majesty are beyond measure, and we are grateful for Your righteous judgment. Help us to respond to Your call to joy with sincerity and whole-hearted worship. May Your joy overflow in our lives, touching those around us and drawing them closer to You. In Jesus' name, Amen.

ALL OF
CREATION
IS BOLDLY PROCLAIMING THE
WONDERFUL
THINGS HE HAS DONE.
LET US JOIN WITH
ALL NATIONS
IN ONE DECLARATION PROCLAIMING THE
GOODNESS OF GOD
LET THE HEAVENS REJOICE AND THE EARTH BE GLAD.
LET THE SEAS RESOUND WITH A
MIGHTY ROAR
LET THE TREES OF THE FOREST
CLAP THEIR HANDS
LET THE EARTH BE FILLED WITH THE
GLORY OF THE LORD

# Wednesday, December 18, 2024

WRITTEN BY GEORGE STONEBERG

Sing praises to the Lord, O you his saints,
and give thanks to his holy name.
For his anger is but for a moment,
and his favor is for a lifetime.
Weeping may tarry for the night,
but joy comes with the morning.
**Psalm 30:4-5**

Have you ever been to a Children's Christmas Program, perhaps with your own children in it? Aren't there always a few kids that sing with abandon, regardless of their skill level, or even ability to carry a tune? Isn't that the very thing which makes it so enjoyable?

God is our Father, and He watches us worship in this season, looking for the same quality in us. So, are you like those kids, anxious to praise and give thanks; or are there worries, problems or troubles that have limited your enjoyment of the season? The Psalmist gives us direction from God; we're to sing praises to the Lord and give thanks to His holy name. Why...because, even when we've angered Him, that anger is brief, while the favor (or blessings) he showers on us lasts throughout our lifetime. Even when things are tough and we feel like we're drowning in sorrow, God reminds us that a joyful morning awaits us.

Blessings and joy are available, but we need to first be sure we have our relationship with our Father in heaven correct. God is not easily angered, but there are things we can do that will trigger it. If you find yourself under God's anger, first and foremost, check to be sure there are no other gods taking His glory. Is your job more important than God? How about your family, your kids and their activities, or even your church responsibilities? Are you stealing His tithe? If any of those are true, repent and make the changes needed and that will stop God's anger in a moment. Then you'll be able to enjoy His favor and blessings.

Do you find yourself in a season of mourning? Our scripture points out that weeping may tarry for the night but joy comes in the morning. What changes to bring about joy...night turning into day. How do we apply that principle to our painful situations? We add the Savior's light into our sad times; He is what makes the difference. Sadly, there are times we decide to be sad by ourselves, that no one else cares or should know of our struggle or even that God caused it. But, that keeps us in the dark, when the path to joy requires injecting the Savior's light into our issues. Godly friends are a great way to do that and being in a group is one of the best way to meet those Godly friends and develop relationships that are deep enough to share troubles. If you find yourself isolated and sad this season, try joining a church growth or home group. You'll be glad you did.

Is this Advent season marked by praise or is there sadness in your life? What changes could you make to bring favor and joy into this time?

## Today's Prayer

Father, thank you for your brief anger and your great favor. Forgive me if I've done anything that angers you and change me to be the person that receives a lifetime of your favor. Help me to remember that your light is what brings joy to a sad situation. Amen.

# PRAISE YOU

WHEN I'M OVERWHELMED
IN MY BROKENNESS
SO I DON'T FORGET

## WHO YOU ARE

## PRAISE YOU

WHEN I'VE LOST MY WAY
WHEN I'M SO AFRAID
'CAUSE IT DON'T CHANGE

## WHO YOU ARE

WEEPING MAY ENDURE FOR THE NIGHT, BUT

## JOY COMES

IN THE MORNING!

# Thursday, December 19, 2024

WRITTEN BY DENNIS DAVIDSON

*You have put more joy in my heart
than they have when their grain and wine abound.*
**Psalm 4:7**

What do you regard as your most prized possession? If it's anything material or physical, you'll never feel truly fulfilled. Scripture confirms this thought. People always seem to be striving to accumulate more and more. We're all seeking some kind of satisfaction.

During this season, you will hear much emphasis on the concept of "joy." The world is constantly longing to experience complete joy. The birth of Jesus is our reminder that joy is not found in our possessions or accomplishments but only in our Savior.

The entire fourth Psalm is a prayer by David and a word to us to trust in the Lord always. He wrote this Psalm as he was being pursued by Absalom to kill him. That would make anyone anxious!

Yet in the 7th verse, David takes inventory of what he has been given — a greater joy than others have who seem to have everything. He is content in spite of fleeing for his life.

What is this "joy?" Many people confuse joy with happiness or an intense feeling of excitement. The Bible doesn't emphasize happiness but joy. Our possessions, accomplishments, even the people in our lives, can make us happy to some extent. Joy is richer than happiness or excitement. Happiness can change with a person's mood or circumstances. Joy, on the other hand, does not depend on our feelings. It is about how we choose to respond and the attitude we have.

So where can we find complete joy? Fullness of joy is found only in God. Psalm 16:11 says "in your presence there is fullness of joy...."

Our relationship with Jesus is our greatest joy. He gives us a joy we cannot find any other way. We are created to be joyful and fully alive. Joy doesn't come from an easy life, but rather from trusting and praising God in every situation.

"I have told you this so that my joy may be in you and that your joy may be complete" (John 15:11 NIV).

What is the result of finding our joy in Jesus? David reminds us in the 8th verse of Psalm 4: "In peace I will both lie down and sleep; for you alone, O Lord, make me dwell in safety."

We will sleep soundly. Instead of pursuing material things that won't last, our greatest joy is found in contentment. When life is based on our relationship with Jesus, we will have more joy than the rest of the world has in their happiest moments. Our soul finds the sweetest and deepest rest — a peace that passes all understanding. What joy!

Have you sought happiness through possessions? Have you thanked God for His greatest gift, Jesus Christ? Place your trust in Jesus and know He alone will give you complete joy — a most prized possession.

## Today's Prayer

Our heavenly Father, we are grateful that with You at the center of our life there is an inner strength and peace, a deep satisfaction, and unfading joy. We commit this season to follow You closer, resting completely in You alone. May this allow us to be fulfilled in greater joy. Thank you for the peace that accompanies this contentment. In our Savior's name, Amen.

# JOY TO THE WORLD

THE LORD IS COME.
LET EARTH RECEIVE HER KING!
LET EV'RY HEART PREPARE HIM ROOM,
AND HEAVEN AND NATURE SING.

# JOY TO THE WORLD

THE SAVIOR REIGNS,
LET ME THEIR SONGS EMPLOY!
WHILE FIELDS AND FLOODS,
ROCKS, HILLS AND PLAINS
REPEAT THE SOUNDING JOY.

# HE RULES THE WORLD

WITH TRUTH AND GRACE
AND MAKES THE NATIONS PROVE
THE GLORIES OF HIS RIGHTEOUSNESS
AND WONDERS OF HIS LOVE.

# Friday, December 20, 2024

WRITTEN BY GINA COOPER

Just so, I tell you, there will be more joy in heaven over one sinner who repents than over ninety-nine righteous persons who need no repentance.
**Luke 15:7**

One morning as I was getting dressed for work, I noticed my wedding ring was not in my jewelry box. I looked by the sink where I had done dishes the evening before. Not there. I looked by my bathroom sink. No ring. I looked by my nightstand for my ring. It was nowhere to be found. I was heartbroken. After a few weeks of trying to find the ring, I finally came to terms that my ring was gone.

Months later we were painting my youngest daughter's bedroom. When we moved her furniture from against the wall, I discovered a mountain of dust bunnies under the bed and something shiny on the floor. It was my ring! I cried tears of joy and immediately placed it back on my finger. I asked my toddler, Lucy, how my ring ended up under her bed and she said she had been sleeping with it every night. I asked her why she would do that. She sweetly replied, "Because Mama, you keep special things close to you." Although I briefly thought about grounding this mischievous child until she graduated high school, I felt such elation in having my wedding ring back, I could not be angry with her. The joy in my heart was just too great!

God feels the same way when one of his precious sheep returns home. He is too overcome with joy to be mad about why they wandered off. God has placed great worth on your life. He decided before you were born that you were worth dying for. It's easy to get caught up in the busyness of the holiday season, but let's take a second to pause and remember why we have the holiday season. It's all about Jesus. He doesn't care about your home being decorated perfectly, your Christmas card being color co-ordinated, or your cookies having the perfect number of sprinkles. He cares about your heart. He wants you to remember him today.

What has my focus been on this season? What can I eliminate so I can make room for Jesus?

## Today's Prayer

Father, I pray for my friend reading this today. I ask that you would remove any distractions from their focus this holiday season. Remind us that you have more joy when we return to you than in our attempts at making everything perfect. Jesus, all of this is for you. Inconvenience us today so we don't miss out on experiencing you. We thank you. We love you. We trust you. We ask this in the name of Jesus. Amen.

THERE WERE NINETY AND NINE THAT SAFELY LAY
IN THE SHELTER OF THE FOLD
BUT ONE WAS OUT ON THE HILLS AWAY FAR OFF
FROM THE GATES OF GOLD
AWAY ON THE MOUNTAINS WILD AND BARE
AWAY FROM THE TENDER SHEPHERD'S CARE
BUT ALL THRO' THE MOUNTAINS THUNDER RIVEN
AND UP FROM THE ROCKY STEEP THERE AROSE
A GLAD CRY TO THE GATE OF HEAVEN
REJOICE I HAVE FOUND MY SHEEP
AND THE ANGELS ECHOED AROUND THE THRONE
REJOICE
REJOICE FOR THE LORD BRINGS BACK HIS OWN!

# Saturday, December 21, 2024
WRITTEN BY JENNIFER BAILEY

Be sober-minded; be watchful. Your adversary the devil prowls around like a roaring lion, seeking someone to devour. Resist him, firm in your faith, knowing that the same kinds of suffering are being experienced by your brotherhood throughout the world.
**1 Peter 5:8-9**

The words of these two verses were penned by Peter, a man who not only saw Jesus, but who also walked with Him daily. As one of the three disciples who were closest to Jesus, Peter knew Him more intimately than most. Centuries later, we could easily imagine that we could never know Jesus as closely as those who actually knew Him, broke bread with Him, walked with Him...those who saw Him. But let us not forget the many who did see Him in the flesh and yet never really understood Him. They did not believe He was who He said He was. Though they saw Him, their lives were not transformed by Him. We have a unique opportunity to read His Word and know Him in a way those who lived during His time never did. John Piper said, "The gospels are better than being there. You are taken into the inner circle of the apostolic band where you never could have gone." If we read His word with our eyes and hearts open and seeking Him, we can truly know Him. Jeremiah 29:13 says, "You will seek me and find me when you seek me with all your heart." He wants us to seek Him. He wants us to find Him.

In this season of advent, seek Him. Look for Him in all the details of your life. God is a God who answers our prayers...our big prayers and our small prayers. These two verses from I Peter 5 remind us of three things.

We are to love Him. Offer your love to Him in word and deed. Pray to Him and tell Him all of the things for which you are thankful He has done. Tell Him the ways you love Him. In this time of year, it is easy to find a way to love oth-

ers. Go and be His hands and feet to those in need around you.

We are to believe and trust in Him. When you cry out to Him, do so from a place of trust, knowing He hears you and will answer your needs. I always tell my children that God does not always give us what we want, but He always meets our needs. Pray with expectation for Him to do the same for you.

We are to rejoice. Be thankful for all He has done for you, most specifically for the gift of salvation. When you see Him come through to meet your needs, do not forget to offer thanks back to Him and rejoice in the Lord.

These are ways we can see Him and know Him. He is waiting to hear from you today, whether He heard from you yesterday or whether it has been weeks or even years since He has heard from you. Let your petitions and requests be made known to God and give yourself an opportunity to truly know Him today.

What is one way you can try to know God better today?

## Today's Prayer

Father, thank you for the revelation of what faith is. How I feel the need of it as I live in the midst of a confused and hopeless society. Grant me the simple faith of a child and teach me to live according to it.

Amen.

SATAN IS LIKE A
ROARING LION
ROAMING TO AND FRO
SEEKING WHO HE MAY DEVOUR
THE BIBLE TELLS US SO
MANY SOULS
HAVE BEEN HIS PREY
TO FALL IN SOME WEAK HOUR
BUT GOD HAS PROMISED US TODAY
HIS OVERCOMING POW'R
GREATER IS HE THAT IS IN ME
THAN HE THAT IS IN THE WORLD.

Sunday, December 22, 2024

# PEACE

## Angel's Candle

We have waited a long time to get to this last Sunday before Christmas. On this fourth and final week of advent we light the last purple candle. It is called the "Angel's Candle", symbolizing peace. It reminds us of the angel's message, "Peace on Earth, Good Will Toward Men." In this frantic and busy season, may we slow down and seek peace that only Jesus can give despite our circumstances and the season surrounding us. Let us share the peace that passes all understanding with others. And let us remember the Kingdom that is to come where peace will reign and the King of Kings will be glorified forever.

Read: Revelation 21:1-4 and 22-27

Sing: Hark the Herald Angels and The First Noel

# Monday, December 23, 2024

For to us a child is born, to us a son is given; and the government shall be upon his shoulder, and his name shall be called Wonderful Counselor, Mighty God, Everlasting Father, Prince of Peace.

**Isaiah 9:6**

As we stand on the threshold of Christmas Eve, Isaiah's prophetic words echo through the centuries, resonating deeply with our hearts today. In a world often characterized by turmoil and uncertainty, the promise of a Prince of Peace offers a beacon of hope and a balm for our weary souls.

The title "Prince of Peace" is particularly poignant in our current times. We live in an era where peace seems increasingly elusive - from global conflicts and political divisions to personal struggles and the relentless pace of modern life. Yet, in the midst of this chaos, we are promised a leader who not only brings peace but embodies it in His very nature.

This peace that Christ offers is far more profound than merely the absence of conflict. It's a deep, abiding sense of wholeness, well-being, and harmony. In Hebrew, this concept is known as "shalom" - a peace that permeates every aspect of our being and our relationships. It's a peace that, as Paul describes in Philippians 4:7, "surpasses all understanding" and has the power to guard our hearts and minds.

As we prepare our hearts for the celebration of Christ's birth, let's reflect on how we can embody this peace in our own lives. How can we be agents of Christ's peace in our families, workplaces, and communities? It might mean extending forgiveness to someone who has hurt us, offering a listening ear to a friend in need, or simply taking a moment to breathe deeply and center ourselves in God's presence amidst the holiday rush.

Remember, the peace that Christ brings is not dependent on our circumstances. It's a gift freely given, available to us even in the midst of life's storms. Just as Jesus calmed the tempestuous sea with a word, He can speak peace into the turbulent areas of our lives.

In these final moments of Advent, let's also consider how we can share this peace with others. In a world starved for genuine peace, we have the opportunity to offer a taste of God's shalom to those around us. A kind word, a generous act, a moment of undivided attention - these can all be channels through which Christ's peace flows to others.

## Today's Prayer

Prince of Peace, as we stand on the brink of celebrating Your birth, fill our hearts with Your perfect peace. Help us to be instruments of Your peace in our homes, workplaces, and communities. May we reflect Your love and bring calm to the chaos around us. Thank You for the gift of Your presence and the promise of eternal peace. In Jesus' name,

Amen.

PEACE! PEACE!

# WONDERFUL PEACE!

COMING DOWN FROM THE

# FATHER ABOVE;

SWEEP OVER MY SPIRIT FOREVER I PRAY.

IN FATHOMLESS

# BILLOWS OF LOVE

WONDERFUL PEACE – W.D. CORNELL

# Tuesday, December 24, 2024

Glory to God in the highest, and on earth peace among
those with whom he is pleased!
**Luke 2:14**

On this Christmas Eve, we find ourselves standing at the threshold of a miraculous event. The simplicity of Luke's words belies the extraordinary nature of what they describe - the birth of the Savior of the world in the humblest of circumstances.

The contrast is stark: the King of Kings, born not in a palace but in a stable; the Lord of Lords, cradled not in fine linens but in rough swaddling clothes; the Prince of Peace, announced not to nobility but to lowly shepherds. This juxtaposition invites us to reflect on the nature of God's kingdom and His ways, which are so often contrary to our human expectations.

In the midst of our often hectic Christmas Eve preparations - the last-minute gift wrapping, the food preparation, the excited anticipation of children - let's take a moment to consider the quiet, humble scene of that first Christmas night. Despite the lack of worldly comforts or recognition, there was a profound sense of rightness, of things falling into place according to God's perfect plan.

This scene challenges our notions of what's truly important. In a world that often equates worth with wealth, status, or influence, the nativity reminds us that God's value system is fundamentally different. He chose to enter our world not as a powerful ruler, but as a vulnerable infant. Not in a place of prominence, but in obscurity. Not with fanfare, but in near silence, save for a choir of angels singing to a handful of shepherds.

What does this mean for us today? It invites us to reconsider our priorities, especially during this holiday season. Are we caught up in creating the perfect Christmas experience, or are we open to finding Christ in unexpected places? Are we so busy with our plans that we, like the innkeeper, have no room for Jesus?

The humble circumstances of Christ's birth also remind us of His accessibility to all. No one is too lowly or insignificant for His attention. Just as the shepherds were welcomed to His birthplace, so too are we all invited to approach Him, regardless of our status or situation in life.

As we prepare our hearts and homes for Christmas Day, let's create space for wonder and simplicity. Perhaps we can take a cue from Mary, who "treasured up all these things, pondering them in her heart" (Luke 2:19). In the midst of our celebrations, let's reserve some quiet moments for reflection, gratitude, and awe at the miracle of the Incarnation.

Let's also consider how we can emulate Christ's humility in our own lives. How can we serve others selflessly? How can we show love to those who might be overlooked or marginalized? How can we, like Jesus, bring hope and joy to unexpected places?

## Today's Prayer

Heavenly Father, on this eve of Your Son's birth, we echo the angels' song of praise. Thank You for the gift of peace that came wrapped in swaddling clothes and lying in a manger. As we celebrate the arrival of Jesus, let Your peace reign in our hearts, homes, and world. May we be bearers of this peace to all we encounter, today and always. In the name of Jesus, our Prince of Peace,

Amen.

O COME, DESIRED NATIONS, BIND

ALL PEOPLES

IN ONE HEART & MIND.

BID ENVY, STRIFE, AND QUARRELS CEASE;

BID ENVY,
STRIFE AND
QUARRELS
CEASE;

FILL THE WHOLE WORLD WITH HEAVENS PEACE,

REJOICE!
REJOICE!

EMMANUEL SHALL COME TO THEE,

O ISRAEL!

# MERRY CHRISTMAS FROM THE CROSS CHURCH!

THE**CROSS**.COM